a bowlful of

BROTH

a bowlful of
BROTH

nourishing recipes for bone broths
and other restorative soups

with recipes &
introduction by
MIRANDA BALLARD

RYLAND PETERS & SMALL
LONDON • NEW YORK

Designer Paul Stradling

Editor Kate Eddison

Production Manager Gordana Simakovic

Art Director Leslie Harrington

Editorial Director Julia Charles

Publisher Cindy Richards

Indexer Vanessa Bird

First published in 2015 by
Ryland Peters & Small
20–21 Jockey's Fields
London WC1R 4BW
and
341 E 116th St
New York NY 10029

www.rylandpeters.com

Text © Miranda Ballard, Amy Ruth Finegold,
Tonia George, Brian Glover, Dunja Gulin,
Jennifer Joyce, Uyen Luu, Elsa Petersen-
Schepelern, Fiona Smith, Laura Washburn,
Belinda Williams, and Ryland Peters & Small
2015

Design and photographs © Ryland Peters &
Small 2015

ISBN: 978-1-84975-685-3

10 9 8 7 6 5 4 3 2 1

A CIP record for this book is available from the
British Library.

US Library of Congress Cataloging-in-
Publication data has been applied for.

Printed and bound in China

NOTES

- Both British (Metric) and American (Imperial plus US cups) measurements are included in these recipes for your convenience; however it is important to work with one set of measurements and not alternate between the two within a recipe.

- All spoon measurements are level unless otherwise specified.

- All herbs are fresh unless otherwise specified.

- All fruit and vegetables should be washed thoroughly before consumption. Unwaxed citrus fruits should be used whenever possible.

- All eggs are medium (UK) or large (US), unless specified as large, in which case US extra-large should be used. Uncooked or partially cooked eggs should not be served to the very old, frail, young children, pregnant women or those with compromised immune systems.

- Ovens should be preheated to the specified temperatures. We recommend using an oven thermometer. If using a fan-assisted oven, adjust temperatures according to the manufacturer's instructions.

CONTENTS

INTRODUCTION

Cooks all around the world have made nutritious broths with vegetables, meat, poultry and fish for centuries. They are perfect for using up leftovers and harnessing vitamins and minerals for health and vitality. Broth is made by simmering bones, meat, fish, poultry or vegetables in water. After a short cooking time, you have a classic stock, but after a long period of simmering, you will be left with a broth that is full of nutrients.

Broth is basically slow-boiled vegetables, animal cuts or bones with seasoning. It can be used as a drink, a flavouring, the base of a soup or stew, or for medicine, and its health benefits are enormous.

Traditionally, the term 'stock' or 'bouillon' describes the strained or reduced liquid which remains after boiling, the term 'aspic' describes the chilled stock or 'set jelly' form, whereas 'broth' was generally the liquid-form with the solid pieces still in it. They all originate with the same process though. Vegetable broth and stock use the slow-boiling method to break down the starches and nutrients in vegetables, and meat and fish broths break down the nutrients in bones and meat.

The taste of broth can add flavour and depth to nearly all cooked meals, and the strained product can easily be stored (refrigerated for up to a week or frozen for up to six months), so you can make it in batches. You can reduce the broth to a thick jelly (see Basic beef broth, page 10) to spoon into a risotto, for example, or strain it to its rich liquid form, freeze it in an ice cube tray, and throw the small portions into a casserole, gravy, sauce, bowl of rice and so on. Remember, our taste buds are designed to react to the flavoursome contents of broth, so this will make you and your guests enjoy their meal even more.

It can also be enjoyed as a soup or drunk as a hot 'tea' and because we have broken down or 'diluted' the minerals, proteins and collagens, our bodies absorb its contents immediately with very little demand for digestion.

Interestingly, because humans share the same ancestry wherever we are in the world, it's no coincidence that cultures were developing their own styles for producing the same range of products. In Japan, for example, 'dashi' is the fish stock base, now becoming very popular around the rest of the world for being combined with another form of a vegetable stock called, 'miso'. In South America, too, for example, Peru has a concentrated fish stock called, 'timbuche' and Russia and Ukraine have a traditional dish using the chilled – 'set jelly' (or 'aspic') – of pork and chicken bones, called 'kholodets'.

In this book, there are basic recipes for meat, poultry, fish and vegetable broths, as well as dashi and miso. Most of the recipes that follow can be made using one of the home-made broths as a base, but feel free to substitute for a different broth if you prefer. You can also use these broths as a basis for a risotto, stew, casserole or any other dish that calls for stock or bouillon. Broth is a simple, usable, nutritious staple in a healthy kitchen and a wonderful addition of flavour to a modern diet.

BONE broth

It's a very modern condition to be squeamish about bones. When meat was reared and slaughtered to the demand of the community around it, we used every part of the animal. From an ethical point of view, this honours the reason the animal was alive and well looked after in the first place. From an economical point of view, why would we throw anything away?

What's more, why would we throw away the parts of the animal that can offer more nutritional bounty than a steak-cut of muscle?

What happens when we boil bones?

Three reactions happen when we boil bones:
1. the dilution of the proteins in the marrow within the bones;
2. the release of all the minerals in the bone mass;
3. the breakdown – or melting – of the proteins and collagen in the connective tissue surrounding it.

The rich meat or fish flavour from these three reactions is sublime. It tastes good to us because we have receptors on our tongue tuned to react to it. We react to it for the simple reason that our body wants what's in it; it's 'tasty' because our body wants it. Indeed, there is a multi-million dollar industry built on a product designed to trick these receptors in the same way for a lot less time and money, it's called monosodium glutamate (MSG) and it does nothing for us.

Why is bone broth good for us?

As well as being really tasty and adding flavour to our recipes, bone broth is so often recommended as part of a good diet, and even more so as a remedy for its 'healing power'. Scientifically, this isn't wrong. We joke about how chicken soup is a go-to prescription when we have the flu but the slow boiling of chicken stock releases an amino acid, called cysteine, which strengthens the immune system and sends a trigger to the body to thin the build up of mucus.

Our modern diets are often lacking calcium, magnesium and phosphorus as we use these up very quickly for growth and consume them at a rate faster than we're replacing them – because of diet. Bone broth is packed full of these minerals and, diluted to liquid form, they are sent flying through the body to be absorbed by the bones, connective muscle and tissue that needs them. There is a huge range of health, beauty and medical benefits that range from treating and preventing osteoporosis, IBS, scurvy, liver and digestive diseases to improving skin, teeth and oral health. To help repair our connective tissues, for example for joint pain or cellulite, we absorb the collagens in the muscle and connective tissue – now called gelatin in its food form – from the bone broth and transform the amino acids into proteins for our bodies.

Briefly, our bodies evolved during a long history of a carnivorous diet. Whatever your food choices today, there is a fundamental, ancestral need for certain nutrients to make our bodies function. There are supplements, of course, and medicines but for the general upkeep of these nutritional needs, there are bones… at no more than a few pence/cents per kg/lb., in fact usually priced at: 'free to a good home'. That's a lot cheaper than protein and mineral supplements and modern pharmaceuticals.

How do we get the best out of our bones?

A great tip to get the best out of your bone broth is to add 2–3 tablespoons apple cider vinegar to the pan. This ingredient helps to break down the connective tissue even more easily, producing extra collagen and proteins in the finished liquid. These are what helps the broth to thicken and the melted collagen will then set when it's chilled.

What type of bones should you use?

Simple – you can use any carcass you like. There are bones with more connective tissue, such as leg bones (for example pork 'hocks', beef 'shin' or lamb 'shank'), which have smaller separate muscles around the bone and therefore they have more connective tissue. There are younger bones with more marrow in, such as veal shin ('osso bucco'), but even a mature beef rack of ribs will be packed full of marrow (and red blood cells/haemoglobin). Fish and chicken have smaller bones, which will soften so much with enough cooking time (more than 8 hours) that they can be crushed or whizzed up in the food processor so you can consume the lot.

How about vegetables and herbs?

For the vegetables and herbs, take the same approach as the meat – no trimming nor aesthetics required! The 'mirepoix' is the very popular combination of celery, white onion and carrot and I use these as part of every broth I make. Keeping the peel of the carrot on is actually better than trimming it, as the starch quantity in the peel is high and will thicken your broth. The stalks of celery and fresh herbs carry more nutrients and flavour than the more easily digestible celery sticks/ribs and leaves of herbs, so these should be used in the

broth too. Don't worry about how they look – you will be straining them out once they have served their purpose. You can choose what herbs and flavourings you want to add – strong herbs like fresh fennel go with beef, dill is delicious with fish, and a little lemon juice and peel added to chicken broth will add more vitamins and a citric 'zing' to the flavour.

Do we need to add salt?

It's up to you if you add salt. Sadly, many of the store-bought stock cubes and bouillon are packed full of salt, so making your own broth and stock is a better way to control the amount you consume. A diet without too much mass-produced or processed food will happily welcome a little salt in the good food you make at home.

BASIC BEEF *broth*

15 g/1 tablespoon butter

3 celery sticks/ribs, including stalks, roughly chopped

3 whole carrots, untrimmed and roughly chopped

2 white onions, roughly chopped

2 garlic cloves, roughly chopped

4–5 beef rib bones, chopped into single bone pieces

the flat, sawn bone ('chine') from the underside of the joint (optional; this may have been removed already, but throw this in the pan if you have it)

a big pinch of cracked black pepper

a pinch of sea salt

2 bay leaves

a sprig of fresh thyme and/or fresh fennel

2 tablespoons apple cider vinegar

MAKES 500–750 ML/2–3 CUPS

Rib bones are a fail-safe cut for beef broth, because they're big, surrounded by connective tissue and full of great marrow. However, you can use any other beef bones you have to hand, of course. You can start with raw bones — ask your butcher or meat shop — or you can roast a rib joint on the bone, carve and eat, and then still use the bones after. They will have released a little of the marrow and collagen but will still be packed full of minerals and proteins and have that extra-lovely flavour from the juices released from the muscle while it was roasting.

Heat the butter in a large saucepan or pot over high heat. Throw in the celery, carrots, onions and garlic, and stir in the melted butter for just 1–2 minutes, until it begins to brown.

Add the bones and all the seasoning, then the apple cider vinegar and enough water to come 2.5 cm/1 inch above the bones. Keep the heat to high to bring to the boil for 10 minutes and then reduce the heat to the lowest setting, half cover with the lid and simmer for at least 4 hours, or 8–10 hours if you can.

If you have a slow cooker, brown the veg in a separate pan and then transfer it with all the ingredients to your pot and keep it on simmer for as long as you like.

Check the pan every hour and top up the water if it's dropped below half the height of the solid ingredients and bones. Stir the mixture as well to make sure it isn't catching on the bottom.

Remove from the heat and strain into a container to cool. Use it straight away as stock, a hot drink or soup, or portion it into bags or containers to refrigerate or freeze. The liquid will thicken to a jelly when chilled. (Alternatively, scoop out the solid ingredients and bones and boil the liquid hard for 15–20 minutes until the liquid starts to thicken even when hot. This will chill to a more solid jelly or 'aspic' with the extra boiling at the end if you would like that.)

BASIC CHICKEN *broth*

the carcass of 1 whole chicken

1 whole lemon, quartered (optional)

4 garlic cloves, roughly chopped (optional)

a pinch of sea salt

a big pinch of cracked black pepper

2 tablespoons olive oil

1 tablespoon apple cider vinegar

1 white onion, roughly chopped

1 carrot, untrimmed and roughly chopped

1 celery stick/rib, including stalks and roughly chopped

a handful of fresh parsley, untrimmed

MAKES 250 ML/1 CUP

Chickens are small – they have lots of little bones and lots of little muscles, perfect for broth. Roasting the carcass with optional ingredients like garlic and lemon is such a good way to add even richer flavour to your broth. These additions are ideal if you're using it as a cooking ingredient for something like chicken casserole, or with other dishes like fish pie or pork stroganoff... anything that would pair well with this combination. If you want a simpler chicken broth, leave out the lemon and garlic.

Preheat the oven to 190°C (375°F) Gas 5.

Place the chicken bones in a roasting pan and then scatter the lemon and garlic around, if using. Add the salt and pepper and drizzle the olive oil on top. Roast, uncovered, in the preheated oven for 30 minutes.

Bring 1.5 litres/quarts water to the boil in a pan with the apple cider vinegar. Add all the contents of your roasting pan along with the onion, carrot, celery and parsley. Reduce the heat to a simmer, half cover with the lid and leave for at least 3 hours, and up to 6 hours if you have the time. Check it every hour and add more water if it drops below half the height of the solid ingredients.

Stir occasionally so that nothing catches on the bottom. If you get dark grey solids and fats on the surface, skim with a metal sieve/strainer or just mix it back in for now, you'll be straining it later so these will be removed.

Remove from the heat and strain into a container to cool. Use it straight away as stock, a hot drink or soup, or portion it into bags or containers to refrigerate or freeze. The liquid will thicken to a jelly when chilled. You can also freeze it in an ice cube tray to portion it for easy use.

BASIC FISH *broth*

50 g/3½ tablespoons butter

2 garlic cloves

12 shallots

1 leek, thickly sliced

2 kg/4½ lbs. white fish carcass/bones (not oily fish or salmon), heads and all but no guts

4 celery sticks/ribs, including stalks, roughly chopped

½ fennel bulb, halved

2 carrots, peeled and thickly sliced

a large bunch of fresh tarragon

a large bunch of fresh parsley

10 black or white peppercorns

sea salt

MAKES 1.5 LITRES/QUARTS

Broths are not just for using up big meaty bones or leftover roast chicken carcasses. Making a delicate fish broth is a fantastic way to use up the bones and heads from white fish. Fish broth doesn't take as long to cook as meat broth, as the bones are more delicate. If you are planning to use it in Asian-style recipes, you can replace the tarragon and parsley with some aromatics such as chillies/chiles, lemongrass, ginger or galangal.

Melt the butter in a large saucepan or pot and add the garlic, shallots and leek. Cook for a few minutes until softened.

Add the fish bones to the pan and top up with 2 litres/quarts water. Add the celery, fennel, carrots, herbs and peppercorns, and bring to the boil. Half cover with the lid and then reduce to a simmer and simmer very gently for at least 1 hour, removing the lid for the last 20 minutes so that it can reduce a little.

Remove from the heat and strain into a container to cool. Use it straight away as stock or portion it into bags or containers to refrigerate or freeze.

BASIC VEGETABLE *broth*

2 onions, halved

2 leeks, thickly sliced

1 fennel bulb, halved

4 celery sticks/ribs, thickly sliced

4 carrots, peeled and thickly sliced

1–2 bay leaves

a few sprigs of fresh thyme

a small bunch of fresh parsley

10 white peppercorns

sea salt

MAKES ABOUT 1.5 LITRES/QUARTS

Making your own vegetable broth at home is simple, inexpensive and the results are far superior to salty stock cubes bought in supermarkets. You can use whatever vegetables and herbs you happen to have to hand, but onions, carrots and celery are always a good choice to act as the base. This broth can be used for myriad vegetable soups, stews, risottos or sauces, and it is packed full of goodness from all those delicious vegetables.

Put all the ingredients in a large saucepan or pot and top up with 2.5 litres/quarts water. Cover the pan with a lid, bring to the boil then reduce to a simmer. Let it simmer for 1½ hours, removing the lid for the last 30 minutes of cooking time so it can reduce a little.

Remove from the heat and strain into a container to cool. Use it straight away as stock or portion it into bags or containers to refrigerate or freeze.

Tip: If you prefer a slightly richer flavour, brown the vegetables in a tablespoon of butter before adding the liquid to the pan.

DASHI *broth*

500 g/1 lb 2 oz. fleshy fish bones

2 tablespoons dried fish or 1 tablespoon bonito flakes

5-cm/2-inch piece of kombu

MAKES 1.5 LITRES/QUARTS

A good dashi, or soup stock, is the basis for any great miso soup. A very simple version requires only kombu and water, but fresh and dried fish give an exceptional result. Little dried fish are sold in packets in Japanese and other Asian supermarkets. Many miso pastes come pre-mixed with dashi, so check the packet if you are adding this dashi to a miso paste — you will need to use a pure miso paste. See below to use your home-made dashi in a classic miso soup.

To make the dashi, put the fish bones, dried fish and kombu in a large saucepan or stockpot, then add 3 litres/quarts water. Bring to the boil, then reduce the heat to a simmer. Simmer, partially covered with a lid, for 2 hours, skimming any foam off the top from time to time.

Strain and use immediately, or cool and store in the refrigerator for up to 2 days or freeze for up to 3 months.

COMBINATION MISO SOUP

To make the soup, put 2 tablespoons each of red miso and white miso paste in a small bowl. Add 4 tablespoons dashi and stir well. Pour 1 litre/quart dashi into a saucepan, bring to the boil, reduce to a simmer and stir in the miso mixture. Return to simmering point, but do not boil. Serve in 4 small bowls.

VIETNAMESE BEEF NOODLE *broth*

600 g/1 lb. 5 oz. boneless oxtail, chopped

1.5 kg/3 lbs. 5 oz. beef shin, flank or rib

700 g/1 lb. 9 oz. beef bones

2 litres/quarts Basic chicken broth (page 11)

1 large onion, trimmed

200 g/7 oz. fresh ginger, peeled

1 daikon/mooli, peeled

a spice bundle of 20 star anise, ½ teaspoon cloves, 3 cassia bark sticks, 2 cinnamon sticks, 1 teaspoon coriander seeds, 1 teaspoon fennel seeds, 1 teaspoon black peppercorns, 2 black cardamom pods and 4 pieces of dried orange peel, tied into muslin/cheesecloth

50 g/1¾ oz. rock sugar

3 teaspoons pork bouillon

4 tablespoons fish sauce

1 red onion, thinly sliced

a small handful of coriander/cilantro

2 spring onions/scallions, thinly sliced

4 portions fresh noodles, blanched

beef fillet/tenderloin, thinly sliced

freshly sliced Thai sweet basil and coriander/cilantro, chopped fresh chillies/chiles, lime wedges, beansprouts, hoisin sauce and chilli/chili sauce, to garnish

sea salt and freshly ground black pepper

SERVES 6—8

This traditional Vietnamese pho uses lots of spices to add depth of flavour to the broth. It's well worth the time spent making it for an aromatic taste of Asia.

Bring a very large saucepan of water to the boil with 2 tablespoons salt. Add the meat and bones and boil until scum forms on the surface – about 10 minutes. Remove from the heat and discard the water. Wash the meat in cold water, removing any scum, and set aside. This will give you a clearer broth.

Wash the pan, add 3 litres/quarts fresh water and bring to the boil. Now add the rested meat and bring to a gentle simmer. Skim off any scum and fat from the surface with a spoon. Add the chicken broth. Now heat a stove-top griddle pan over high heat. Char the onion and ginger on both sides. Add to the broth with the daikon/mooli. Add the muslin/cheesecloth spice bundle to the broth with 3 tablespoons salt and the sugar. Simmer for at least 2 hours with the lid on. Check it occasionally and skim off any scum and fat from the surface.

After 2 hours, remove the beef from the pan and allow it to rest slightly, then slice it thinly and store it in a sealed container until serving. Leave the bones and oxtail in the pan and simmer for at least 1 hour more. When ready to serve, add the pork bouillon, fish sauce and some black pepper, to taste.

Mix together the red onion, coriander/cilantro and spring onions/scallions. Place a portion of cooked noodles into a big, deep soup bowl with a pinch of black pepper. Place some cooked beef on top and sprinkle with the red-onion mixture. To make it special, add raw beef fillet/tenderloin (it will cook perfectly in the hot broth). Bring the broth to boiling point, then pour ladles of it over the noodles to submerge them. Serve with the selection of condiments and garnishes for each diner to add.

SPICED LAMB SHANK BROTH
with redcurrant & rosemary

1½ teaspoons cumin seeds

2 tablespoons olive oil

2 lamb shanks

2 large onions, roughly diced

2 garlic cloves, chopped

2 sprigs of fresh rosemary, plus extra to serve

1 cinnamon stick

4 green cardamom pods

5–7-cm/2–2¾-inch piece of fresh ginger, grated

1.5 litres/quarts Basic vegetable broth (page 13)

½ bottle red wine

2 carrots, peeled and sliced

2 celery sticks/ribs, sliced

3 tablespoons redcurrant jelly

a squeeze of fresh lemon juice (optional)

sea salt and freshly ground black pepper

SERVES 6

This is a two-stage process; first, you need to cook the lamb to impart the spice to the broth, which is then used to form the base for the soup. If you like a slightly thicker base to your soups, break up some chunky stale white bread and add this a few minutes before serving to thicken it in an authentic fashion.

Dry roast the cumin seeds in a frying pan/skillet for a couple of minutes over medium heat to release their flavour, then set aside to cool.

Heat the oil in a large saucepan or pot, add the lamb shanks and brown them over high heat. Add the onions, garlic, rosemary, spices and ginger and pour over the broth and red wine. Cover with the lid and simmer for 2 hours.

When the lamb is very tender, remove the shanks from the pan and set aside to cool. Strain the broth into a clean pan. If it looks at all fatty, allow to cool and skim well. Tear the lamb into nice generous pieces, but not too large to be too much of a mouthful.

Put the broth back over medium heat and add the carrots, celery, redcurrant jelly and lamb pieces. Bring the liquid to a simmer, then reduce the heat to low and gently cook until all the vegetables are tender – about 20 minutes. Remove the sprigs of rosemary and season with plenty of black pepper and a little salt. Add a squeeze of lemon juice to sharpen the flavour, if you wish.

Ladle the soup into bowls and serve garnished with extra sprigs of fresh rosemary.

CASSOULET-STYLE BROTH *with*
chipolatas, beans & ham

300 g/10½ oz. chipolatas or other thin sausages

2 tablespoons olive oil

6 shallots, quartered

4 garlic cloves, sliced

100 g/3½ oz. Speck ham or thick-sliced back bacon, cut into large thick lardons

250 g/9 oz. butternut squash, diced

4 celery sticks/ribs, sliced

70 g/5 tablespoons tomato purée/paste

800 ml/3⅓ cups Basic beef broth (page 10) or Basic chicken broth (page 11)

400 g/14 oz. canned chopped tomatoes

a good glug of red wine (optional)

a bouquet garni made up of fresh thyme, bay leaves and good few sprigs of fresh parsley

200 g/7 oz. mixed canned beans, such as haricot/navy or butter/lima beans (use whatever are your favourites), drained

a large handful of long French beans

a handful of fresh parsley, chopped

a handful of fresh thyme sprigs, leaves only

sea salt and freshly ground black pepper

SERVES 6

Excellent sausages are produced in France, but there are also fantastic locally produced sausages to be found in the UK and USA. Use whatever good-quality sausages you can find. Thin ones (herby chipolatas are especially good) that have been cooked under the grill/broiler are the best, as the colour and caramelization of the skin adds to the dish and gives it a slightly smoky flavour. Cut them on an angle and leave quite large, as this is supposed to be a hearty broth, and all the ingredients need to be kept chunky and honest!

Cook the chipolatas under a grill/broiler until evenly browned. Leave to cool, then slice them on an angle into large chunks.

Put the oil in a heavy-based saucepan, throw in the shallots, garlic and ham, and cook until all just beginning to brown, but do not over-colour.

Add the squash, celery and tomato purée/paste, then top up with the broth, tomatoes and wine, if using. Add the bouquet garni, put the lid on the pan and leave to simmer for 25 minutes.

Add the canned beans, green beans and sausages and cook for a further 3–4 minutes to heat through. Season with salt and black pepper, then sprinkle over the fresh herbs and serve.

SLOW ROAST BELLY PORK, *noodles & shiitake mushrooms in sour broth*

400-g/14-oz. piece of belly pork

2 tablespoons vegetable oil

½ red onion, very finely sliced

2.5-cm/1-inch piece of fresh ginger, peeled and finely sliced into thin strips

150 g/5½ oz. shiitake or mixed exotic Chinese mushrooms

250 ml/1 cup canned beef consommé

1.5 litres/quarts Basic chicken broth (page 11)

200 g/7 oz. soba or other buckwheat noodles

2–3 fresh green chillies/chiles, deseeded and finely sliced

4 spring onions/scallions, sliced on the angle and whites and greens separated

2 teaspoons sesame oil

2 tablespoons mirin (Japanese rice wine)

2 tablespoons soy sauce, plus extra to taste

3–4 tablespoons rice vinegar, plus extra to taste

150 g/5½ oz. canned water chestnuts, drained and sliced

2 heads of pak choi/bok choy

SERVES 6–8

This is one of those soups that you know will taste good because it looks a bit intriguing: a clear broth of great flavours and textures. It is packed full of delicious and wholesome ingredients. The crunch of the water chestnuts is a wonderful contrast to the slippery nature of the mushrooms. The mixture of rich, sweet, salty and sour is typical of Chinese food, and this soup demonstrates all these characteristics brilliantly.

Preheat the oven to 220°C (425°F) Gas 7.

Put the pork belly in a greased roasting pan and roast for 30 minutes, then turn the temperature down to 180°C (350°F) Gas 4 and roast for a further 30 minutes.

Pour off any fat, remove the crackling (and reserve for the garnish, if you like) and cut the meat into even slices. Set aside.

Heat the oil in a large saucepan, add the onion and ginger, and toss over medium heat until softened. Add the mushrooms to the pan and stir to coat with the oil. Pour in the consommé and broth, and bring the liquid to a simmer. Add the noodles, chillies/chiles, spring onion/scallion whites and pork slices, and simmer for 5–7 minutes, until the noodles are tender.

Add the sesame oil, mirin, soy sauce, rice vinegar and water chestnuts. Adjust the seasoning by adding more soy sauce and vinegar. When happy with the balance of sweet, salt and sour, add the spring onion/scallion greens and the pak choi/bok choy and cook for a further 2 minutes.

Serve in Chinese bowls, garnished with pieces of crackling, if using.

CLASSIC CHICKEN NOODLE *broth*

2 tablespoons olive oil

1.4 kg/3 lbs. chicken drumsticks and thighs

1 onion, chopped

1 carrot, peeled and chopped

1 garlic clove, sliced

2 celery sticks/ribs, chopped

a bouquet garni made up of fresh bay leaves, thyme and parsley

TO FINISH

1 onion, chopped

2 large carrots, peeled and sliced 1 cm/ ½ inch thick

2 celery sticks/ribs, sliced 2.5 cm/ 1 inch thick

90 g/3 oz. fine Jewish egg noodles, broken into pieces

20 g/1 oz. fresh parsley, finely chopped

sea salt and freshly ground black pepper

SERVES 4

The trick to producing a rich broth is to brown the chicken first and cover while simmering. The result is a deep, flavoursome base which suits any additions. For this recipe, you make your broth as you cook your chicken, but you can use the Basic chicken broth (page 11) and use leftover cooked chicken instead. Fine Jewish egg noodles are classic, but you can try rice or matzo balls.

Heat 1 tablespoon of the olive oil in a large, heavy stockpot. Season the chicken pieces and brown them in the stockpot in batches. Put all the chicken pieces back in the pot with the onion, carrot, garlic and celery, and cook over low heat for 15 minutes. Pour in 1.5 litres/quarts water, add the bouquet garni and simmer, covered, for 1 hour over medium–low heat. Remove any foamy scum from the surface during cooking.

Strain the finished stock through a fine sieve/strainer into a bowl and skim off any excess fat. Reserve the chicken and let cool before removing the meat from the bones and roughly chopping it.

To finish, heat the remaining olive oil in a pan. Add the onion, carrots and celery, and season. Sauté for 5 minutes, then pour in the stock. Bring to the boil and add the noodles. Cook until the noodles are al dente, then add the chopped chicken. Sprinkle in the chopped parsley, stir and serve.

ROAST CHICKEN, *garlic & watercress broth*

a whole 1.2-kg/2¾-lb. chicken

3 whole garlic bulbs

300 g/10½ oz. baking potatoes

2 tablespoons extra virgin olive oil, plus extra to serve

6 fresh thyme sprigs

900 ml/4 cups Basic chicken broth (page 11)

150 g/5½ oz. watercress

sea salt and freshly ground black pepper

SERVES 4

You can either honour this soup by roasting a chicken especially for the occasion or you can buy a rotisserie chicken. Of course, if you've had a roast, providing you haven't picked every last bit of meat from it, it's a good way to use that up, too. There's nothing more satisfying than two meals from one bird; it makes one feel very thrifty and clever.

Preheat the oven to 200°C (400°F) Gas 6.

Place the chicken in a roasting pan, wrap the garlic bulbs and potato in foil individually and place around the edges. Drizzle the olive oil over the chicken, scatter the thyme sprigs over the top and season well. Roast in the preheated oven for 1 hour.

Open the packages of roasted garlic and potato to allow them to cool off and, at the same time, check that they are really soft inside. If not, return to the oven for a little longer until soft. Pull the chicken meat from the carcass and keep the carcass for your next batch of chicken broth. Hopefully, you should have some chicken broth ready to go, but if not you can use the carcass to whip up a batch (see page 11).

Pour the broth into a large saucepan. Discard the skin from the potato, chop the flesh and add it to the pan. Cut the tops off the garlic bulbs, squeeze out the soft flesh from inside the cloves and add to the soup. Chop up the chicken meat and add that to the soup too. Transfer about one-third of the soup to a blender along with the watercress, and liquidize until smooth. Return to the pan and stir until blended. Add more water if you think it's too thick. Season to taste.

Divide the soup between serving bowls and drizzle with extra olive oil.

CHICKEN BROTH *with* *black forbidden rice*

a whole 1.2-kg/2¾-lb. chicken, cut into 8 pieces

1.5 litres/quarts Basic chicken broth (page 11)

2 carrots, peeled and chopped

1 celery stick/rib, chopped

130 g/1 cup cooked black rice (cook according to packet instructions)

chopped fresh parsley and dill, to garnish

SERVES 4

Black rice has its origin in China. It has a pleasantly mild, nutty flavour and its colour makes for striking presentation. This recipe honours the children's book author, Maurice Sendak, 'cooking once, cooking twice, cooking chicken soup with rice!' You can also use leftover cooked chicken in your Basic chicken broth, rather than cooking a whole chicken, if you like. However, just add it to the broth at the end to heat through, so that it doesn't overcook.

Put the chicken in a large saucepan or pot with the chicken broth over a medium–high heat and bring to the boil. Reduce the heat, cover and simmer for 1 hour.

Remove the white breast meat so that it doesn't overcook and set aside in the refrigerator. Return the bones to the pan and simmer for another hour. Strain the broth and discard the bones. Shred the chicken into bite-size pieces.

Skim the fat off the top of the broth and pour into a large saucepan or pot. Add in the chopped carrots and celery, and the black rice. Cook until the vegetables are tender, then add the shredded chicken and cook until heated through. Serve immediately, garnished with chopped parsley and dill.

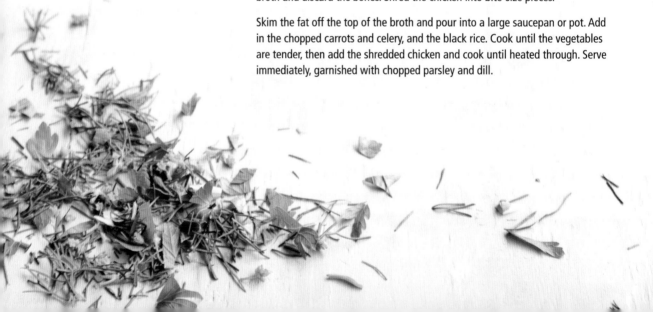

CHICKEN BROTH *with vegetables*

a whole 1.2-kg/2¾-lb. chicken

2 whole star anise

2 cinnamon sticks

a handful of kaffir lime leaves

2 lemongrass stalks, halved lengthways and bruised

7-cm/3-inch piece of fresh ginger, peeled and sliced

4 garlic cloves, lightly crushed but whole

1 fresh red chilli/chile, halved lengthways

1 tablespoon peppercorns, bruised

a handful of mini asparagus tips, halved crossways

a large handful of sugar snap peas, cut into 2–3 pieces each

1 punnet cherry tomatoes, quartered and deseeded

sea salt and freshly ground black pepper

fresh coriander/cilantro leaves, to garnish

SERVES 4

The basis of this soup is one of the simplest, best, most flavourful chicken broths in the world – an Asian stock to rival the legendary Jewish mother's chicken soup. The better the chicken, the better the stock, so invest in organic, free-range and all those desirable things.

Put the chicken in a large saucepan with the star anise, cinnamon, kaffir lime leaves, lemongrass, ginger, garlic, chilli/chile and peppercorns. Add water to cover the chicken by 3 cm/1¼ inches, bring to the boil, reduce the heat and simmer for at least 1 hour.

Remove the chicken and ginger from the pan. Remove the white breast meat from the carcass and set aside. Cut the ginger into tiny slivers and set aside. Put the bones back in the pan and cook the broth for a further 3 hours, or longer if you have time.

Strain the broth into a saucepan, ladling at first, then pouring through muslin/ cheesecloth. It should be clear but slightly fatty on top. The fat is typical of Asian broths, but you can skim it off, if you prefer.

Taste the broth and season to taste. Shred the chicken into bite-size pieces.

Return the broth to the boil, add the ginger slivers and thick parts of the asparagus and blanch for 30 seconds. Add the tips and blanch for 3 seconds more. Add the peas, tomato quarters and chicken, and blanch for 30 seconds. You are heating them and keeping the peas and tomatoes fresh, rather than cooking them to a mush. Ladle into large soup bowls and top with fresh coriander/cilantro leaves. Serve immeditaely.

HEAVENLY VEGETABLE BROTH
with chicken & kaffir lime

1 tablespoon very light vegetable oil

4 boneless, skinless chicken breasts, sliced into thin strips

8 spring onions/scallions, finely sliced and whites and greens separated

3 garlic cloves, crushed

2 fresh green chillies/chiles, finely diced

2 lemongrass stalks, bruised

800 ml/3⅓ cups Basic vegetable broth (page 13)

6 kaffir lime leaves

1 small leek, white only, finely sliced

8 celery sticks/ribs, finely sliced

2 fennel bulbs, finely sliced

1 courgette/zucchini, finely sliced

200 g/1½ cups fresh or frozen peas

200 g/1⅓ cups skinned baby broad/fava or edamame beans

grated zest and freshly squeezed juice of 1½ limes, or to taste

a handful each of fresh parsley, coriander/cilantro and mint, chopped

sea salt

SERVES 6

Oh my goodness, how can something this good for you taste so incredible? Almost fat-free, fresh as a summer garden and as aromatic as having your nose in a lime tree! This is just the most heavenly little creation in the entire world. If you like a little Asian influence, this one is for you!

Pour the oil into a large saucepan, pop in the chicken breasts while the oil is still cold and stir to coat well. There is very little oil, so a fine coating on the chicken before the heat takes hold will prevent it sticking to the pan, and breaking up. (We don't want that, as this soup needs to be almost a clear broth with every exquisite element holding its own.)

As the pan begins to take heat, add the spring onion/scallion whites, garlic, green chillies/chiles and lemongrass. Toss around the pan for a couple of minutes, until the chicken becomes white around the outside, then pour on the vegetable broth. Add the lime leaves, leek, celery and fennel. Cover the pan and cook over gentle heat for about 7–10 minutes, until the fennel becomes tender but not too soft. This soup needs to keep a little crunch.

At this point, remove the lime leaves and lemongrass if you feel their job is done, or leave them in if you want to make these flavours more pronounced.

Add the courgette/zucchini, peas and beans and cook for a further 3–5 minutes, until tender. Add the lime zest and half of the lime juice, taste, then add the rest of the juice if you feel it needs it, then season with a little salt. Stir in the fresh herbs.

Serve immediately, scattered with the sliced spring onion/scallion greens.

RED LENTIL BROTH *with chicken, fresh turmeric & chilli*

120 ml/½ cup ground nut or vegetable oil

4 boneless, skinless chicken breasts

2 onions, diced

2 carrots, peeled and diced

2 sweet potatoes, peeled and diced

5-cm/2-inch piece of fresh turmeric, grated (or 1 teaspoon ground turmeric)

1 fresh red chilli/chile, deseeded and very finely sliced

1–2 teaspoons red curry paste, to taste

4 garlic cloves, crushed

100 g/½ cup red lentils, rinsed

80 g/½ cup sultanas/golden raisins (optional)

2 litres/quarts Basic chicken broth (page 11)

sea salt and freshly ground black pepper

leaves from a good bunch of fresh coriander/cilantro, to serve

SERVES 6–8

There is no doubt that if you can find the gnarly little stems of fresh turmeric they make this soup far superior. The root looks very much like slim ginger, but is, as you would expect, deep reddish orange in the centre. It has heat, but also an aromatic pungent flavour, and is a great addition if you can track it down. Dried turmeric is a good second best, so do try this soup anyway.

Put the oil in large saucepan set over high heat and add the chicken breasts to the pan in a single layer. Cook for a couple of minutes, until browned, then turn them over and brown them on the other side. Reduce the temperature and cook for about 10 minutes until firm and cooked through, then remove the chicken from the pan and set aside.

Add the onions, carrots and sweet potatoes to the pan and cook over medium heat until just beginning to take colour, stirring occasionally. Add the turmeric, chilli/chile (reserve a little, for the garnish), curry paste and garlic and cook, stirring, for a further minute.

Add the lentils, sultanas/golden raisins, if using, and stock to the pan and bring to a simmer. Put the lid on the pan and allow the broth to cook for 20 minutes or so, until the vegetables and lentils are tender.

Slice or roughly chop the chicken and add it back to the soup. Simmer for a further 10 minutes without the pan lid to reduce the liquid slightly and make the broth a little thicker. When all the ingredients have fused in colour and flavour and the sultanas/golden raisins are swollen, season to taste.

Ladle the soup into large bowls, garnish with the reserved chilli/chile and fresh coriander/cilantro leaves, and serve.

SPICY CITRUS BROTH
with prawns

2 litres/quarts Basic fish broth (page 12)

6 lemongrass stalks, bruised

2 fresh red chillies/chiles, split (seeds and all)

8 kaffir lime leaves

2 tablespoons sliced fresh ginger

8 spring onions/scallions, sliced

2–3 tablespoons peanut/groundnut oil

500 g/1 lb. 2 oz. raw green king prawns/ jumbo shrimp, shelled

3 garlic cloves, finely sliced

1 fresh green and 1 fresh red chilli/chile, finely diced

250 g/9 oz. straw or mixed Chinese mushrooms, finely sliced

10 spring onions/scallions, sliced, whites and greens separated

4–5 tablespoons fish sauce

1–2 tablespoons soy sauce

freshly squeezed juice of 1 lime

a handful of fresh coriander/cilantro leaves

200 g/7 oz. mangetout/snow peas or sugar snap peas, sliced on the angle

sea salt and freshly ground black pepper

lime wedges, to serve

SERVES 6

This is such a fresh and healthy broth, it almost does you good just to read the recipe! It will give you a glow in your cheeks and leave you feeling energized and ready to go. You can try it with any other shellfish or firm white fish too. If you cannot find straw mushrooms, use shiitake or another variety of Chinese mushroom – the weirder they look, the better the soup will look!

Put the fish broth in a large saucepan or pot and add the lemongrass, split red chillies/chiles, 6 of the kaffir lime leaves, 1 tablespoon of the ginger and the 8 spring onions/scallions. Bring the liquid to a simmer. Continue to simmer for 15 minutes or so with the pan covered, until an aromatic infusion has been achieved, then pass the broth through a sieve/strainer to remove the seasonings.

Heat the oil in a large saucepan and add the prawns/shrimp along with the garlic, remaining ginger, green and red chillies/chiles and mushrooms. Toss around until all are well coated in the oil and cook for about 3–5 minutes, until the prawns/ shrimp are beginning to turn pink. Pour over the broth, then add the remaining 2 lime leaves, the spring onion/scallion whites, fish sauce and soy sauce, and simmer for a further 3–5 minutes.

Add most of the lime juice, taste and then add more lime juice or soy sauce if you feel the seasoning is not sufficient. When happy with the flavour – the soup should be hot, salty and sour – stir in the coriander/cilantro, spring onion/scallion greens and mangetout/snow peas or sugar snap peas. Ladle generous servings of the broth into bowls and serve with lime wedges on the side.

TOM YUM

2 litres/quarts Basic fish broth (page 12) or Basic vegetable broth (page 13)

4 tablespoons fish paste

1 onion, roughly diced

4 lemongrass stalks, bruised

6 kaffir lime leaves

2–3 bird's eye chillies/chiles, finely sliced

1 kg/2¼ lbs. mixed fresh fish, prawns/shrimp or squid, cleaned, scaled and cut into chunks

4 spring onions/scallions, finely sliced

2 tablespoons freshly shaved coconut (optional)

2 heads of pak choi/bok choy, sliced

6 tablespoons fish sauce

2 teaspoons mirin (Japanese rice wine) or ½ teaspoon soft brown sugar

freshly squeezed juice of 2 limes

a small bunch of fresh coriander/cilantro, torn

SERVES 6

This Tom Yum is a very quick Thai-influenced soup that can be made with either a fish or vegetable broth, depending on what you have to hand. You can alter the fish and shellfish according to taste, too, making it a very adaptable dish.

Pour the broth into a large saucepan or pot and add the fish paste, onion, lemongrass, lime leaves and 2 of the chillies. Bring the mixture to a simmer over medium heat and cook for about 20 minutes. Pour the mixture through a sieve/strainer, discarding the solids.

Transfer the broth to a clean saucepan or pot and bring to a simmer, then add the fish and seafood, spring onions/scallions and shaved coconut. Cook for about 5–7 minutes over medium heat, until the fish and seafood are just cooked.

Add the pak choi/bok choy. Season with the fish sauce and mirin. If you want a little more heat and colour, add another finely sliced chilli/chile. Adjust the acidity with the fresh lime juice, adding a little at a time until you are happy with the flavour. Finally, stir in the torn fresh coriander/cilantro.

Ladle the soup into bowls and serve immediately.

HOT & SOUR BROTH *with prawns*

450 g/1 lb. large raw prawns/jumbo shrimp

1 tablespoon sunflower or peanut/
groundnut oil

1 teaspoon grated lime zest

1.25 litres/quarts Basic fish broth (page 12)
or Basic chicken broth (page 11)

2 lemongrass stalks, thinly sliced

3 garlic cloves, halved

2.5-cm/1-inch piece of fresh ginger,
unpeeled and sliced

a small bunch of fresh coriander/cilantro,
chopped, stalks reserved

3 kaffir lime leaves

a bunch of spring onions/scallions, thinly
sliced, whites and greens separated

2–3 fresh red chillies/chiles, halved
and deseeded

1 large carrot, cut into matchstick strips

2–3 tablespoons Thai fish sauce

freshly squeezed juice of up to 2 limes

1–2 pinches of caster/granulated sugar

180 g/6½ oz. Asian greens, such as pak choi/
bok choy or mustard greens, sliced

sea salt and freshly ground black pepper

lime wedges, to serve

SERVES 4

It's the lime juice and kaffir lime leaves that make this hot and sour soup so addictively delicious. The lime cuts through the heat of the chilli/chile and counterbalances the salty piquancy of the other essential ingredient – Thai fish sauce, or nam pla. While prawns/shrimp work particularly well here, you could also use strips of flash-fried squid or strips of white fish.

Shell and devein the prawns/shrimp, then toss 8–12 of them in the oil with the lime zest and season with a little salt. Roughly chop the remainder into 3–4 pieces each. Set aside all the prawns/shrimp in the refrigerator.

Put the broth, lemongrass, garlic, ginger, coriander/cilantro stalks, kaffir lime leaves, the green parts of the spring onions/scallions and 1–2 chillies/chiles in a saucepan or pot, bring to the boil and simmer, covered, over medium heat for 15–20 minutes. Strain and return to the pan.

Add the carrot and cook for 3–4 minutes, then add the white part of the spring onions/scallions and the chopped prawns/shrimp. Simmer for a few minutes, then add fish sauce and lime juice to taste. Adjust the seasoning with salt, pepper and a pinch or two of sugar. The soup should be fairly piquant and sharp.

Meanwhile, heat a ridged stove-top grill pan or frying pan/skillet until hot, add the reserved whole prawns/shrimp and quickly fry them for 2–3 minutes, until they turn pink and opaque.

Reheat the broth if necessary and stir in the Asian greens and most of the coriander/cilantro leaves. Ladle the hot soup into bowls and add 2–3 whole prawns/shrimp to each bowl. Garnish with the remaining coriander/cilantro leaves and remaining chilli/chile, shredded, then serve with lime wedges.

FISH BROTH

3 red (bell) peppers

2 tablespoons extra virgin olive oil

½ fennel bulb, finely chopped

1 onion, finely chopped

6 garlic cloves, sliced

1 tablespoon cumin seeds, toasted in a dry frying pan/skillet and crushed

½ teaspoon cayenne pepper

1 teaspoon sweet smoked paprika

2 tomatoes, skinned, deseeded and chopped

1 tablespoon tomato purée/paste

2 potatoes, about 600 g/1 lb. 5 oz., peeled and diced

a pinch of saffron threads, soaked in about 4 tablespoons boiling water

120 ml/½ cup dry white wine

1.25 litres/quarts Basic fish broth (page 12)

a bouquet garni made up of a few sprigs of fresh thyme and a bay leaf

350 g/12 oz. monkfish, cut in pieces

350 g/12 oz. boneless halibut, cut in pieces

275 g/10 oz. boneless sea bass fillets, cut in pieces

a small handful of fresh parsley, chopped

sea salt and freshly ground black pepper

a baking sheet lined with kitchen foil

SERVES 4

The flavours in this recipe are a little bit French (fennel and saffron) and a little bit Spanish (peppers, cumin, paprika), so anything you serve with this dish can come from either side of the border. The choice of fish is deliberate because a mix of textures makes for the best fish broths. You could use prawns/shrimp in place of the halibut and add 500 g/18 oz. fresh mussels instead. Despite a long list, this comes together quite quickly. Begin by roasting the (bell) peppers, toasting the cumin and preparing the vegetables, and the rest will easily fall into place.

Preheat the oven to 220°C (425°F) Gas 7.

Rub the (bell) peppers lightly with oil, arrange on the prepared baking sheet and roast in the preheated oven until wrinkled and charred, about 40 minutes.

Remove from the oven, wrap up in the foil and set aside for about 20 minutes. Remove the peppers from the foil, slip off the skins, deseed and chop coarsely.

Put the remaining oil, fennel and onion in a large saucepan or pot over medium heat and cook for 3–5 minutes, or until soft. Season with salt and pepper, then add the garlic, cumin, cayenne and paprika. Cook for 1 minute, stirring constantly. Add the tomatoes, tomato purée/paste, potatoes, and the saffron and its soaking water. Mix well.

Add the wine and fish broth. Add the bouquet garni to the pan. Bring to the boil, then simmer gently until the potatoes are just tender, about 15 minutes. Add salt and pepper to taste.

Add the peppers and fish and simmer until they are cooked through, about 5 minutes. Add the chopped parsley and serve immediately.

LENTIL, SPINACH *& cumin broth*

3 tablespoons extra virgin olive oil

2 onions, sliced

4 garlic cloves, sliced

1 teaspoon ground coriander

1 teaspoon cumin seeds

150 g/¾ cup brown or green lentils

1.25 litres/quarts Basic vegetable broth (page 13)

200 g/7 oz. spinach

freshly squeezed juice of 1 lemon

sea salt and freshly ground black pepper

TO SERVE

4 tablespoons Greek yogurt

25 g/1 oz. pine nuts, lightly toasted

SERVES 4

This is Lebanese in origin, but soups like this are served all over the Middle East. Crispy fried onions are a lovely topping, but you have to be brave and really brown them so they look almost black. In order to do this without burning them, you have to really soften them to start with.

Heat the extra virgin olive oil in a large, heavy-based saucepan or pot and add the onions. Cook, covered, for 8–10 minutes until softened. Remove half the onion and set aside.

Continue to cook the onion left in the pan for a further 10 minutes until deep brown, sweet and caramelized. Take out and set aside to use for the garnish.

Return the softened onion to the pan and add the garlic, coriander, cumin seeds and lentils and stir for 1–2 minutes until well coated in oil. Add the broth, bring to the boil then turn down to a gentle simmer for 30 minutes until the lentils are lovely and soft.

Add the spinach and stir until wilted. Transfer half the soup to a blender and liquidize until you have a purée. Stir back into the soup. Season with lemon juice, sea salt and freshly ground black pepper.

Divide the soup between serving bowls, add a dollop of Greek yogurt, and scatter the pine nuts and fried onions over the top.

COURGETTE, BROAD BEAN
& lemon broth

2 tablespoons extra virgin olive oil

1 lemon

1 onion, chopped

3 tablespoons chopped fresh parsley, plus extra to serve

500 g/1 lb. 2 oz. courgettes/zucchini, sliced

300 g/10½ oz. broad/fava beans (podded weight)

800 ml/3⅓ cups basic vegetable broth (page 13)

sea salt and freshly ground black pepper

LEMON AND THYME OIL

2 lemons

2 fresh thyme or lemon thyme sprigs

250 ml/1 cup extra virgin olive oil

SERVES 4

To make this broth more substantial, you could add a scoop of risotto rice at the same time as the broad/fava beans and a little more broth to compensate. If you are using large beans you might want to slip them out of their pale green jackets, but this is a real labour of love!

To make the lemon and thyme oil, peel off the lemon zest using a peeler, leaving behind the bitter white pith. Put the zest, thyme and olive oil in a saucepan or pot and heat gently for 10 minutes. Remove from the heat and leave to cool. Season to taste.

Heat the olive oil in a large saucepan or pot. Peel the zest from the lemon in one large piece so it's easy to find later and add that to the pan. Add the onion, parsley and courgettes/zucchini, cover and cook over low heat, stirring occasionally, for about 8 minutes or until softening.

Remove the lemon zest. Add the broad/fava beans and broth, season well and return to the heat for a further 20 minutes.

Transfer one-quarter of the soup to a blender, liquidize until smooth, then stir back into the soup. Check the seasoning and add lemon juice to taste.

Divide the soup between serving bowls, drizzle with lemon and thyme oil and serve with extra parsley and a fresh grinding of black pepper.

MINESTRONE

2 tablespoons olive oil

4 rashers/slices of bacon, chopped (or vegetarian bacon, if making this dish vegetarian)

1 large onion, diced

3 carrots, peeled and diced

1 celery stick/rib, sliced

1 leek, sliced

3 potatoes, peeled and diced

2 garlic cloves, crushed

400 g/14 oz. canned chopped tomatoes

1.5 litres/quarts Basic vegetable broth (page 13)

a handful (about 70 g/2½ oz.) of broken spaghetti, or similar

400 g/14oz. canned cannellini or haricot/navy beans, drained

250 g/9 oz. spinach or other greens, chopped

1–2 courgettes/zucchini, diced

a bunch of fresh parsley, chopped

1 teaspoon mixed dried herbs

paprika, to taste (optional)

sea salt and freshly ground black pepper

freshly grated Parmesan cheese (or vegetarian Italian-style hard cheese, if making this dish vegetarian), to serve

SERVES 6

The Italian classic minestrone is a hearty broth that is enriched with vegetables, beans and pasta. This vegetable broth has the addition of some bacon for flavour, but you can use a vegetarian substitute or omit it altogether if you are serving this dish to vegetarians.

Heat the olive oil in a large saucepan or pot and fry the bacon over medium heat until browned. Add the onion, carrots, celery, leek and potatoes, put the lid on the pan and sweat for a few minutes over gentle heat, until the vegetables soften without colouring.

Add the garlic to the pan and continue cooking for a few minutes before adding the chopped tomatoes, stock and pasta. Bring the liquid to the boil, then reduce to a simmer and cook until the vegetables are just tender and the pasta is almost cooked. Add the beans, greens, courgettes/zucchini and parsley to the pan and continue to cook for a few minutes until the greens are tender but still green. Season to taste with salt and freshly ground black pepper and, if you like a little heat, stir in a little paprika.

Serve generous portions of the soup in big flat bowls and finish with lots of freshly grated Parmesan cheese.

MUSTARD GREENS & TOFU *broth*

1 litre/quart Basic vegetable broth (page 13)

100 g/1 cup cubed fresh tofu

2-cm/1-inch piece of fresh ginger, julienned

1 spring onion/scallion, thinly sliced

a dash of vegetable oil

a pinch of sugar

sea salt and freshly ground black pepper

300 g/10½ oz. Chinese mustard greens, chopped

SERVES 2 AS A MAIN/ENTRÉE OR 6 AS AN APPETIZER

This is a great palate-cleansing soup to be had with an array of dishes at lunch or dinner with family or a few friends. The leaves can be consumed at any time and the refreshing broth can be slurped from your bowl in between rice servings. Sometimes it is great to add ramen to the broth for a midnight snack.

Bring the broth to the boil in a saucepan. Add the tofu, ginger, spring onion/scallion, oil, sugar and a pinch of salt and pepper.

When you are ready to serve the soup, add the Chinese mustard greens to the pan and bring to the boil again.

Serve hot by itself as a main meal or with an array of other dishes and rice.

Alternatively, you can add spinach, watercress, pak choi/bok choy or choi sum instead of Chinese mustard greens. It is also absolutely irresistible as a noodle soup base. Just add a portion of dried ramen or fresh udon noodles and cook for 2–3 minutes.

RED MISO BROTH *with pork & noodles*

200 g/7 oz. buckwheat noodles

1 litre/quart Dashi broth (page 15)

1 small leek, finely sliced

3 tablespoons red miso paste

100 g/3½ oz. roast pork, thinly sliced

SERVES 2 AS A MAIN COURSE/ENTRÉE
OR 4 AS AN APPETIZER

This heartier version of miso soup is perfect at the beginning or end of a sushi meal. Serve it before heavier meat- or poultry-based sushi rolls or after delicate fish or vegetarian rolls. It can also be beefed up with stir-fried vegetables as a great big bowl of soup for two.

Fill a large saucepan or pot three-quarters full of water and bring to the boil. Add the buckwheat noodles and return to the boil. Add 250 ml/1 cup of cold water and bring to the boil again. Boil for 3 minutes, drain, rinse in cold water and drain again.

Pour the dashi broth into a saucepan or pot and bring to the boil. Add the leeks and reduce to a simmer. Mix the miso paste in a bowl with a few tablespoons of the dashi broth to loosen it, then stir it into the simmering broth.

Divide the noodles and slices of roast pork between the serving bowls, ladle over the hot soup, then serve.

GRILLED SALMON *noodle broth*

1 tub silken tofu

2 bundles somen or soba noodles

4 large salmon steaks, skin on

2 tablespoons sunflower oil

1 litre/quart Dashi broth (page 15)

your choice of other vegetables, such as sugar snap peas (a large handful per serving)

a handful of Chinese dried mushrooms, such as tree ear (optional), soaked in hot water for 20 minutes

about 6 spring onions/scallions, sliced (optional)

sea salt, fish sauce or soy sauce, to taste (optional)

sliced fresh chillies/chiles or chilli/chili sauce (optional)

SERVES 4

Given some fresh salmon steaks and a kitchen stocked with some pretty basic Asian ingredients, this elegant dinner dish can be on the table in about 8 minutes – or 30 if you're chatting and enjoying yourself over a glass of wine. Add whatever vegetables you have on hand. Tree ear mushrooms have no flavour, just an interesting texture and appearance, and a beautiful name.

To prepare the tofu, put it between 2 plates and put a weight on top (a small can of tuna, for instance). This will force out some of the liquid and make it stick together better. Just before serving, cut into 12 cubes – three cuts one way, four the other.

Bring a large saucepan or pot of water to the boil and add the noodles. Have a glass of cold water ready. When the water comes to the boil, add a dash of cold water. When it returns to the boil, do it again, return to the boil and do it again. This will help cook the noodles perfectly right to the middle – the cold water 'frightens' the heat into the interior. Test after 3–4 minutes, then drain and keep in cold water until ready to serve.

Put the salmon in a plastic bag, add the oil and toss to coat. Bring a stove-top griddle pan or frying pan/skillet to a high heat, then add the salmon, skin-side down. When the skin is charred and the flesh has turned pale about 1 cm/½ inch through, turn the salmon over and lightly sear the other side. It should stay pink except for a line on either side.

Bring the dashi broth to the boil, then lightly blanch your chosen vegetables. Remove with a slotted spoon. Drain the mushrooms and slice into pieces, discarding the hard stalk tip.

Put a pile of drained noodles into each bowl. Put the salmon steaks, skin-side up, on top. Add the tofu cubes, mushrooms and any other vegetables used. Ladle the broth over the top and serve topped with spring onions/scallions, if you like. If you prefer, add seasoning in the form of salt, soy or fish sauce and heat in the form of fresh chillies/chiles or chilli/chili sauce.

HEALING MISO *broth*

7-cm/3-inch piece of dried wakame (seaweed)

2-cm/1-inch piece of fresh ginger

4 spring onions/scallions

110 g/²⁄₃ cup fresh tofu

2 tablespoons sesame oil

4 garlic cloves, crushed

a pinch of salt

480 ml/2 cups hot water

1–2 tablespoons barley or rice miso

2 tablespoons chopped fresh parsley

freshly squeezed juice of ½ lemon

SERVES 2

If you've never had soup for breakfast, you should try treating yourself with a bowl of hot miso soup like this one. In Japan, miso soup is traditionally served for breakfast, accompanied by rice and pickled vegetables. It's very clear why the Japanese have the world's longest life expectancy! Apart from nourishing you with enzymes, vitamins and minerals, this delicious, energizing soup will also support your immune system — perfect if you're suffering from fatigue or the common cold. Don't forget that you can combine different kinds of miso in the same broth! Since hatcho (soy) miso is of high quality but has a strong taste, try to combine ½ tablespoon of soy miso with ½ tablespoon barley miso to get all the benefits of both kinds of soy paste. In warmer weather, you may want to substitute darker miso pastes with the milder sweet white miso.

Soak the wakame in a bowl with 120 ml/½ cup cold water until soft. Drain (reserve the water), cut into small pieces and set aside. Peel the fresh ginger and finely mince half of it. Finely grate the other half in a small bowl and keep for later. Chop the spring onions/scallions, separate the whites and greens, and cut the tofu into small cubes.

In a frying pan/skillet, sauté the white part of the spring onions/scallions for 1 minute in the sesame oil, then add the garlic, ginger and salt. Sauté a little longer, add the hot water, tofu and set-aside wakame and cover. Bring to the boil, then lower the heat and simmer for 4 minutes. Remove from the heat.

Pour approximately 60 ml/¼ cup hot water into a small bowl. Add the miso and purée really well with a fork, until completely dissolved. Pour back, cover and let sit for 2–3 minutes. Take the grated ginger in your hand and squeeze it to release the juice directly into the hot soup. Discard the remaining ginger pulp. Add the chopped spring onion/scallion greens, freshly chopped parsley and lemon juice, and serve immediately!

HEARTY ONE-POT *miso broth*

100 g/3½ oz. dried soba noodles

1 teaspoon salt

½ tablespoon tamari

2½ tablespoons dark sesame oil

3 dried shiitake mushrooms

1 strip wakame seaweed (optional)

1 tablespoon chopped garlic

2 tablespoons chopped fresh ginger

1 small onion, diced

2 carrots, diced (around 100 g/3½ oz. total weight)

120 g/1 generous cup cubed pumpkin

¼ teaspoon ground turmeric

freshly ground black pepper

a pinch of chilli/chili powder

100 g/1½ cups mung bean sprouts

2 tablespoons rice or barley miso

130 g/4½ oz. spinach leaves, chopped

SERVES 3

A big bowl of this soup makes a great lunch, especially when you feel tired and your energy is low. It's also a great late-night dinner option because it nourishes you but doesn't put too much strain on the already sleepy digestive system. Also, dried shiitake mushrooms have a relaxing effect on the body.

In a large saucepan or pot, boil the noodles in 1.25 litres/quarts of salted water until al dente. Strain, reserving the cooking water. Run the noodles through running cold water, drain, put in a bowl and sprinkle with the tamari and ½ tablespoon of dark sesame oil. Mix well and set aside.

In a small bowl, cover the shiitake and wakame, if using, with hot water and leave to soak.

Rinse the saucepan or pot in which you cooked the noodles and add the remaining dark sesame oil. Over a medium heat, sauté the garlic and ginger for 2–3 minutes, then add the onions, carrots, pumpkin cubes and a pinch of salt. Mix well and sauté for 2–3 minutes.

Add the turmeric, pepper and chilli/chili powder and stir. Once the spices and vegetables start sizzling, add the reserved cooking water and another 500 ml/ 2 cups hot water. Cover and bring to the boil over a medium heat. Meanwhile, drain the shiitake and wakame and chop finely, discarding the mushroom stems.

Once the soup has started to boil, add the mung beans, shiitake and wakame, lower the heat and cook, covered, for 10 minutes. Put the miso in a small bowl and pour over a ladle of hot soup. Dilute completely with the help of a small whisk or fork. Remove the soup from the heat and add the diluted miso and chopped spinach. Taste and adjust seasoning. Stir, cover and allow to rest for 1 minute.

Divide the cooked noodles among bowls and pour over the soup, making sure that each portion gets a lot of veggies and sprouts. Serve immediately.

CLEAR JAPANESE BROTH *with*
prawns, citrus & pepper

4 shelled uncooked prawns/shrimp, with tail fins intact

4 thin strips of citrus zest, such as yuzu if available, tied in a knot, or a slice of carrot or other vegetable, blanched

1 litre/quart Dashi broth (page 15), hot but not boiling

4 leaves of Japanese herb, such as shiso, or a slice of spring onion/scallion

furikake seasoning, Japanese seven-spice, or freshly ground black pepper, to serve

SERVES 4

There are three main kinds of Japanese soups; the miso soups with tofu and wakame served as a 'drink' with sushi or sashimi; the big soups, such as New Year Soup; and these — clear dashi in which floats one to three beautiful ingredients, each a complement to the other.

Cut each prawn/shrimp along the belly without cutting all the way through. Open it out flat. Make a small slit where the backbone would be if it were a fish. Thread the tail up and through the slit in the back, then fan out the tail fins.

Cut the citrus zest with a cannelle cutter. Put the zest and prawns in a bowl and pour over boiling water.

Divide the hot dashi broth between serving bowls and add 1 prawn, 1 knot of zest or a slice of vegetable and a herb. Serve with a small dish of furikake seasoning, Japanese seven-spice or black pepper.

INDEX

RECIPE CREDITS

Miranda Ballard
Basic Chicken Broth
Basic Meat Broth

Amy Ruth Finegold
Chicken Broth with Black
    Forbidden Rice

Tonia George
Roast Chicken, Garlic
    & Watercress Broth
Courgette, Broad Bean
    & Lemon Broth
Lentil, Spinach & Cumin
    Broth

Brian Glover
Hot & Sour Broth with
    Prawns

Dunja Gulin
Healing Miso Broth
Hearty One-pot Miso Broth

Jennifer Joyce
Classic Chicken Noodle
    Broth

Uyen Luu
Vietnamese Beef Noodle
    Broth
Mustard Greens & Tofu
    Broth

Elsa Petersen-Schepelern
Chicken Soup Broth
    Vegetables
Clear Japanese Broth with
    Prawns, Citrus & Pepper
Grilled Salmon Noodle Soup

Fiona Smith
Dashi Broth
Red Miso Broth with Pork
    & Noodles

Laura Washburn
Fish Broth

Belinda Williams
Basic Fish Broth
Basic Vegetable Broth
Spiced Lamb Shank Broth
    with Redcurrant
    & Rosemary
Cassoulet Broth of
    Chipolatas, Beans
    & Dry-cured Ham
Slow Roast Belly Pork,
    Noodles & Shiitake
    Mushrooms in Sour Broth
Heavenly Vegetable Broth
    with Chicken & Kafir Lime
    Leaves
Red Lentil Broth with
    Chicken, Fresh Turmeric
    & Chilli
Citrus Broth with Chilli,
    Ginger & King Prawns
Tom Yum
Minestrone

PICTURE CREDITS

Martin Brigdale
Page 25

Peter Cassidy
Pages 3, 5, 30, 54, 61

Richard Jung
Page 41

Diana Miller
Pages 14, 53

David Munns
Page 42

Steve Painter
Pages 9, 18, 21, 22, 33, 34–38, 48–49

William Reavell
Pages 2, 7, 51

Toby Scott
Pages 57, 58

Yuki Sugiura
Pages 26, 45, 46

Ian Wallace
Page 1

Kate Whitaker
Page 4

Clare Winfield
Pages 17, 50

Polly Wreford
Pages 28, 29